EEEEEEEEEEEEEE

Q Pootle 5
NICK BUTTERWORTH

Atheneum Books for Young Readers
New York London Toronto Sydney Singapore

Q Pootle 5 has landed.

He has come to earth. But earth is not where Q Pootle 5 wants to be.

He is on his way to a moon party for his friend Z Pootle 6, but something has gone wrong.

Q Pootle 5 has a problem with his spaceship. One of the rocket boosters won't boost. The spaceship won't fly. Q Pootle 5 looks carefully at the rocket booster.

"Hmm," he says. He thinks he knows what is wrong with it.

"It's just as I thought," he says.

"It's broken."

The spaceship needs a new rocket booster.
But where on earth can he find one?

Ah! Here comes an earthling. Perhaps he knows. He looks friendly and he is a nice color. Green.

"Please can you help?" Q Pootle 5 asks.

"I need a rocket booster."

The earthling can't help. He doesn't even know what a rocket booster is.
Never mind. Here come some more earthlings. Perhaps they can help.

"Excuse me," says Q Pootle 5.
"Do you know where I can find
a new rocket booster?"
The earthlings think
very hard.

"No," says the first one. "Sorry."

"We don't use rocket boosters," says the second.

"We're birds," says the third earthling.

"Oh dear," says Q Pootle 5. "I'm going to be late for the party."

But here comes another earthling.
And look! The earthling is carrying a
rocket booster!
What luck.

"Please," says Q Pootle 5,
"can you help me?"

He tells the earthling about his spaceship
and how it won't fly without a new
rocket booster.
"You can have this one,"
the earthling says.
"As soon as I
finish my dinner."

The earthling is called Henry.

He is pleased to help.

As soon as Henry has finished his dinner
Q Pootle 5 fixes the new rocket booster
onto the spaceship.

Q Pootle 5 climbs into his spaceship.

He presses the starter button,

but nothing happens.

"Oh, beeebotherboootle!" says

Q Pootle 5. "I'm going to be late

and Z Pootle 6 will be upset."

Henry looks carefully at the spaceship.

"I'm not very clever with rockets," he says,

"but I think I can see the problem."

Henry knows why the spaceship won't fly.

"Can you pass me a spoon?" he asks.

"There's a bit of my dinner stuck

in your rocket booster."

Now the rocket booster is clear.

Q Pootle 5 presses the starter button.

There is a rumbling sound, then a BANG!

followed by a funny smell that smells

a bit like Henry's dinner…

only cooked.

Q Pootle 5 pushes the starter button again.
Hooray! The spaceship whooshes up into
the air. Q Pootle 5 waves good-bye to Henry
and the birds and the green earthling.
And they wave back.